AROUND
THE FAL

Carrick Roads and Pendennis as seen from Trelissick on a bright winter afternoon.

First published 1989

by

LANDFALL PUBLICATIONS

Landfall, Penpol, Devoran, Truro, Cornwall TR3 6NW
Telephone: Truro (0872) 862581

Second edition, 1991

British Library Cataloguing in Publication Data
Acton, Bob, *1937-*
Around the Fal : circular walks
I. Title
914.2378

ISBN 1 873443 01 3

★ ★ ★ ★ ★ ★ ★ ★

**THIS BOOK IS FOR MY GRANDSON JAMIE,
just turned four, and already proving himself
a good walker.**

★ ★ ★ ★ ★ ★ ★ ★

MY THANKS TO .....

Peter Gilson, a former teaching colleague, until recently Honorary Librarian of the Royal Cornwall Polytechnic Society, and an authority on this region, who very kindly checked through the whole text and made many useful corrections and additions; Ken Coad, who has lived in Ruan Lanihorne for almost all of his 82 years, and gave up most of a Sunday morning to share with my wife and me his knowledge and memories of the area; the staff at the County Museum, Truro; and, as ever, my wife for her enthusiastic support and her fund of knowledge and ideas.

Typesetting and illustrations by Bob Acton

Printed by the Troutbeck Press
and bound by R. Booth Ltd, Antron Hill, Mabe , Penryn, Cornwall

CONTENTS

(THE WALKS AFFECTED ARE 2, 3, 4, 7, 8 and 10.)

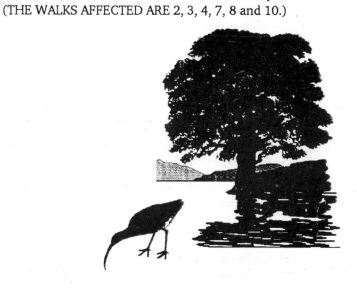

INTRODUCTION

You would be hard put to it to find another region of similar size to the Fal estuary which offers so many beautiful, interesting and varied walks. Peter Gilson of the Royal Cornwall Polytechnic Society believes that it ought to be declared a National Park, and that a footpath should be created around the entire shore. I agree, but would add that in fact we are already fortunate in having ready access for walkers to so much of the shoreline - in comparison, for example, to the Dart in Devon and the Odet in Brittany. Admittedly, there are two large areas which I was not able to include on any of the walks, namely the Tregothnan estate, except the part around Lamorran, and the big parcel of land west and south from Philleigh as far as St Just, which does not seem to lend itself to "round walks". One advantage, though, of the comparative inaccessibility of these two areas is that they remain almost totally "undeveloped" and thus form a marvellous backdrop to the walks on the opposite banks.

I have tried to cater for all tastes and needs of walkers by offering many choices of route. Eight of the ten main walks can be shortened, the exceptions being No. 1, which is already very short, and No. 9, which is only six miles. On the other hand, several tempting diversions are suggested for those with time and energy to spare, and six of the walks can be linked into pairs to provide three full-day excursions. In addition to the basic ten, I have outlined two other very fine round walks by the estuary, referring you to my first book, *A View from Carn Marth,* for details. The same walks are given in updated form and with fuller detail in *A Second View from Carn Marth,* due to be published in June 1991. At the start of each walk description is an outline of the points of interest, together with practical advice on such matters as how to drive to the starting point, where to park, availability of refreshments en route, any special requirements such as waterproof footwear, and arrangements you could consider making beforehand to add to your enjoyment, such as phoning for an appointment to visit the coastguard station at Pendennis.

To the best of my knowledge, all the routes are on public rights of way. Of course, things are always changing: a footbridge collapses, a farmer decides his cows will stray unless he puts up barbed wire, a new housing development is built..... With the help of readers, if they will let me know of any problems not mentioned in my directions, I will try to keep this book up-to-date as long as it remains in print, either by producing a small slip to insert, or by making revisions in any reprint that may be needed.

I hope you will enjoy doing these walks as much as my wife and I have, and if you arm yourself with the relevant O.S. maps you will be able to make further discoveries for yourself.

Bob Acton

May 1989; revised May 1991

SEE PAGE 62 FOR CORRECTIONS AND OTHER REVISIONS MADE IN 1991.

BOB ACTON

AROUND
THE FAL

Falling tide at Coombe, March 1989

Circular Walks

WALK 1

FALMOUTH:
THE DOCKS AND PENDENNIS

*(About one and a half miles,
or just over two if you include
the suggested walk around the Castle moat.)*

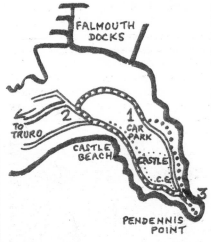

A very short walk – under an hour's gentle strolling – but it's full of beauty and interest, and it leaves you plenty of time to visit Pendennis Castle (Opening hours, 1989-90: 24 March to 30 September, Daily 10 a.m. to 6 p.m.; 1 October to 12 April, Daily except Mondays, 10 a.m. to 4 p.m.) and the important Coastguard Station (strictly speaking, Falmouth Maritime Rescue Co-ordination Centre) which is just south of the castle. Visits to the Centre to see the way things are run in the operations room can be arranged by telephoning the Station Officer, Operations (Falmouth 313053). On the walk you have an amazing bird's-eye view of Falmouth Docks; come on a working day if you can, to see ship-repair work in progress. The walk around Pendennis Point provides magnificent views, firstly over Falmouth's beaches and along the coast beyond the Helford to the Manacles (see the note in Walk 10), and then, after you have reached the headland, of Carrick Roads and Falmouth Harbour. A little road walking is involved, but there is always a footpath beside the road, and on the east side of Pendennis Point there is a well-walked path below the road level. You should have no problems with mud, and refreshments are available in season at the car park, at the Bedruthan Guest House near the drive up to the castle, and probably from ice-cream vans at several strategic points.

Falmouth town itself is, of course, full of interesting and attractive places. I was very tempted to extend this walk to include at least Arwenack House and the waterfront between Custom House Quay and the Prince of Wales Pier, but finally decided against it, partly because that area does not link very conveniently with Pendennis as part of one walk, and also because all you need to help you explore Falmouth is contained in a cheap but well-produced booklet, *Falmouth Town Trail Walkabout* (Cornwall Heritage Project). The same booklet also covers the route I am suggesting here, with an extension to include Gyllyngdune and Fox Rosehill Gardens.

THE HORNWORKS

Chambers' Dictionary defines a hornworks as, "an outwork having angular points or horns, and composed of two demi-bastions joined by a curtain" (i.e. a rampart). In other words, it is an extension to a castle, built to give extra defence, which was needed during the Civil War when the castle was besieged. Little is left now of the Pendennis hornworks.

The directions are given from the large, free Hornworks (*) Car Park. The entrance to it is on Castle Drive, just past the viewing-point above Falmouth Docks. At the car park are toilets and Victor Drago's licensed restaurant, where snacks can be had.

FALMOUTH DOCKS

The foundation stone of the "New Docks" was laid in 1860, just three years before the arrival of the railway; the two together did much to relieve conditions in the town after a period of depression following the departure of the Post Office Packet Ship Service. Of the four main dry docks currently in use, the largest, called Queen Elizabeth Dock, was built in 1953, is 850 feet long, and can take ships up to 100,000 tons - only about one-tenth the size of the largest modern vessels. Until about the 1920s, ship building was a major activity at the Docks (198 vessels were built in all), but since then the work has consisted of repairing and re-fitting. Despite several crises in recent decades, which have seen a great reduction in the workforce, the Docks have a good record of work relations and profitability, and they remain a vital part of Falmouth's economy.

The 'Cutty Sark' in dry dock at Falmouth in 1938, just before she set sail for Greenwich. For several years she had been anchored in Falmouth Harbour and used as a boys' holiday training ship.

1 Before leaving the car park, notice the old water tower not far from the entrance; this substantial building, used until about the end of World War I to supply water to tented camps on the Hornworks, is worth inspecting. From the car park entrance, turn left on Castle Drive, the scenic road around the headland, constructed in 1865. Use the footpath, but cross soon to see Falmouth Docks (*), and also a good view across the Harbour to Falmouth. On the left side of the road here is part of a large oil-storage depot. Continue along the road towards the imposing Falmouth Hotel, built on a narrow neck of land, so that its guests can enjoy views over both bay and harbour.

2 At the T-junction turn left, and then when you reach the coast road (Cliff Road), bear left. To visit Pendennis Castle (*), go up the drive on the left beside the No Entry signs. To continue the walk, go on along the road till you reach Pendennis Point. (The two paths on the right before that, by the way, lead down to the foreshore – a good place to study rock pools.) On the left, where the road curves left round the headland, is the drive up to Falmouth Coastguard Station (*). *(Even if you don't have an appointment to visit this, it's well worth going up the drive in order to get on to the path which goes around the castle moat - a*

PENDENNIS CASTLE

"Pendennis" means "Castle Head"; the name goes back well beyond 1539, when Henry VIII decreed that castles should be built here, at St Mawes, at Trefusis Point and at Gyllyngdune, overlooking Falmouth Bay. A map of 1540 shows an ancient rampart at the neck of the headland; it also shows that work on St Mawes Castle had started, but not yet at Pendennis. However, both castles were complete by 1546; the plans for Trefusis and Gyllyngdune were dropped. The theory was that, since "Black Rock", at the entrance to the harbour, obliged entering ships to steer towards either Pendennis or St Mawes, the guns at those two castles would be able to defend the harbour adequately. In 1598, Queen Elizabeth I had the Pendennis ramparts strengthened, a deep dry ditch excavated and new gun batteries added, so that when it was besieged during the Civil War (1646) it held out for five months and eventually surrendered only because of famine; the Governor, Sir John Arundell, and his garrison of 900 were allowed to march out with honours. The castle was occupied by the army as part of the coastal defences during both World Wars. Apart from the buildings themselves and the magnificent views to be had, attractions for visitors include a museum with a good collection of weapons and armour. One of the more modern buildings within the Castle complex is now used as a Youth Hostel.

FALMOUTH COASTGUARD STATION

Falmouth is one of six Coastguard Maritime Rescue Coordination Centres in Britain; the others are at Swansea, Clyde, Aberdeen, Yarmouth and Dover. To quote from an official leaflet: "Rescue Centres keep a constant radio watch on the international distress frequencies and also handle telephone, telex and facsimile messages through specially designed consoles. Each Centre has a fully fitted operations room with emergency planning, press and staff facilities, along with storage for rescue equipment, vehicles and boats." The Falmouth Centre covers the coastline from Tintagel to Dodman Point, and 650,000 square miles of sea, as far as 15°W longitude.

LITTLE DENNIS BLOCKHOUSE

Little Dennis seems to have been built a few years before the castle itself as part of a defensive site which covered the whole of the southern end of the headland. The blockhouse originally had four guns at ground level and others on the roof. Notice how, as on the castle, the battlements lean inwards to lessen the impact of shot. Inside, you can see the holes which once carried the big beam supporting the roof; the fireplace and oven show that the garrison actually lived and fed here.

Little Dennis. Black Rock and St Anthony Lighthouse in the distance.

delightful walk with superb views. Continue past the entrance to the Coastguard Station, and where the track curves left go straight on along the narrow path, which soon brings you out on top of the bank surrounding the moat. This curves left beside the Hornworks car park, so you could return to your car this way to shorten the walk if you wish. Otherwise, take the path on the left at the edge of the car park; this brings you to the road leading up to the castle entrance. Walk up to the ticket kiosk and continue along the bank-top path from there. Soon you reach a well-preserved double gun emplacement, used in both the World Wars; from there, pass between the three wooden posts to return to the track that passes the Coastguard Station entrance.) Out on Pendennis Point, it's worth going down on the east (harbour) side to look at Little Dennis Blockhouse (*).

3   From there, take the footpath which runs along the cliff edge and then turns inland around two inlets (known in Cornwall as "zawns", from the Cornish *sawn*, a cleft or gully; the same word explains the name of Zone Point, near St Anthony). The opening on the right leads to the remains of an old quay and a World War II gun emplacement; bear left of this. The footpath now runs below and more-or-less parallel with the road. Later, keep to the lower path, passing a picnic table. Soon you reach the road, but the path continues on the right. Now you have a view ahead of derelict-looking land which is the site of the proposed Falmouth Container Terminal, a scheme whose many local opponents say it would have a drastic effect on the estuary, changing conditions in ways hard to predict accurately both for wildlife and also for sailors, oyster fishermen and other users of the rivers and creeks. Other objections often expressed are that local land communications would be inadequate to handle the increased traffic, and that few extra permanent jobs for local people would flow from the project. Less controversially – the bluebells along here are a splendid sight in May, and the rabbits seem remarkably tame. The path returns you to the road opposite the car park entrance.

WALK 2

MYLOR BRIDGE, PENRYN AND FLUSHING
(About eight miles.
Details are given at the end of the directions
of a shorter walk starting at Mylor or Flushing.)

Quite a long walk, but beautiful scenery and many points of
interest amply repay the effort involved. Penryn is among
Cornwall's most historic towns, and this walk shows you
clearly what made it once so important; Flushing is a
picturesque village where fish is still landed; and Mylor
harbour, formerly the smallest Royal Naval Dockyard in the
world, is now a mecca for yachtsmen, as well as having a
church to rival St Just-in-Roseland. (See Walk 8.) Linking
these is a lovely waterside path with fine views, first over
Falmouth Harbour, then across Carrick Roads, and lastly along
Mylor Creek. The short inland section is also attractive,
passing through the estates of Enys House. You may well find
muddy patches, especially inland and approaching Little
Falmouth and Trefusis Point, but the going in general is easy.
Besides Mylor Bridge, pubs and shops are available at Penryn
(though not quite on the walk route suggested) and Flushing,
and refreshments can be had at Mylor harbour in the season.
If you would enjoy a twelve-mile walk, you could join this one
to Walk 3. In that case, I suggest you start with Walk 3,
because slightly less road walking is involved that way. The
easiest way to link the two is described at the end of Walk 3,
and for convenience I have placed the sketch-map for both at
the start of that walk.

To drive to Mylor Bridge from Truro, take the A39 south towards
Falmouth. About a mile and a half past Carnon Downs, watch for
the Norway Inn on the right, and take the left turning immediately
beyond it; from here, Mylor Bridge is signposted. Coming from
Falmouth on the A39, turn right in Penryn where signposted to
Mylor Bridge and Flushing, just beyond the Volvo showrooms. The
main car park in Mylor is just off the main street, on the same
side as the Lemon Arms. There are also buses to Mylor Bridge from
Falmouth and Penryn.

1 From the car park, turn left up Lemon Hill, and then left again
along Comfort Road. After passing the 30 m.p.h. derestriction sign,
go on for another few hundred yards and take the first surfaced
road on the left, Broads Lane, signposted Elim Cottage (*).

2 About 200 yards along Broads Lane, take the first main left turning
(a wide, stony track), where there are field entrances and the
remains of a gate. Go straight on where another track crosses.

9

MYLOR BRIDGE

This village, attractively situated at the head of Mylor Creek, is a favourite choice for retirement homes, and has grown quickly in recent years. The earliest mention of a village here was in the 17th Century. In 1785 the whole of it became part of the Carclew estate, owned by the Lemon family: hence the prominence of that name in the village. See the note on Carclew in Walk 3. There was an inn called the Griffin at least as far back as 1765; by 1821 this was the Red Lion; and by 1837 a new building, closer to the road, was called the Lemon Arms. These details, plus many more about the chapel, poor-house and schools, can be found in an interesting article in *History around the Fal*, Part 3. Sheila Bird writes of the boatbuilding at Mylor Bridge, and also of some literary connections: Katherine Mansfield and John Middleton Murry lived here for a while after staying with D.H. and Frieda Lawrence at Zennor; and Howard Spring had a bungalow here.

ELIM COTTAGE

Elim Cottage has very lovely gardens which are occasionally opened to the public in aid of charity.

ENYS

A large estate with famous gardens, unfortunately very rarely open to visitors, although you can catch several glimpses of them from the path. The Enys family have lived here since before the Domesday survey, but the present house dates only from about 1800.

3 Now watch for a stile on your left, with a sign about keeping dogs on a lead. Cross this stile, and from now on you will be guided all the way to Penryn by the yellow arrows of the Country Landowners Association and/or Public Footpath signs. During this part of the walk you are skirting the extensive grounds of Enys (*). You cross a small stream on entering woodland, and go straight on at the clearing (tractor-ruts). Where a lane crosses, go left then immediately right through a gate. At the next gate cross the drive and follow the yellow arrow by the left-hand granite post. The path goes to the right of Gwarder farm. After the next gate, keep by the hedge on the left. (Enys Gardens are to your right now - and beyond the lodge is a wood intriguingly named Horneywink.) After another gate, follow the footpath sign left to Pencoose. (*Coose* or *Goose* in Cornish place names refers to a wood.) After the farm, the lane brings you down to a road at the edge of Penryn.

4 Turn left and then take the footpath on the right, signed "The Causeway". Keep to the right of the new block of garages, and go on down the path where it resumes — again signposted "The Causeway". This brings you out opposite the Volvo showrooms.

5 Turn left on the road signposted to Mylor Bridge and Flushing. Soon this brings you to St Gluvias Church (*). When you are ready to walk on, go to the right of the church, where the waterside path begins, near two metal gates. To your right across the river are the boatyards and old warehouses of Penryn (*), with its clock tower and granite houses. After Penryn Quay come the modern

---

ST GLUVIAS CHURCH

St Gluvias is the parish church of Penryn. It appears to mark the site of one of the earliest Celtic settlements around here. Parts of the church — notably the tower — date from the 15th Century, but most of the old building was destroyed during a harsh restoration in 1883. According to Sheila Bird, another bit was lost when French sailors took the main door to replace the rudder of their ship.

St Gluvias Church, Penryn, in the snow

PENRYN

Penryn is one of Cornwall's oldest towns, granted its charter in 1265, long before Falmouth was anything more than a word on maps, denoting the harbour. Almost nothing is left of Glasney, the great Collegiate Church dissolved in 1547, but there are still plenty of old buildings, many of them beautifully restored since 1975, when Penryn became a Housing Action Area because so much of the older part of the town had deteriorated to the level of a slum. Falmouth's rise helped to cause the decline of Penryn, and there is still much rivalry between the two. From the Exchequer Quay tin, granite and oysters were shipped, and imports included cattle from Spain. (As with Falmouth and Truro, an adequate note on Penryn would at least double the size of this book, and since I'm aiming to produce something easily portable it's better to refer you to the Further Reading list.)

industrial buildings along the Penryn-Falmouth road. Soon after the reedy inlet you come to metal gates, with Trevissome House to your left and Falmouth Marina on the far shore. Then comes your first sight of Falmouth Docks with Pendennis Castle behind. As you leave the next inlet, the path becomes very boggy, but you can walk along the edge of the field above it and then continue beside the hedge on your left.

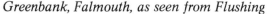

Greenbank, Falmouth, as seen from Flushing

LITTLE FALMOUTH

Once there was a pilchard processing plant at Little Falmouth, but since the late 17th Century it has been a shipbuilding and repair yard. The first dry dock in the harbour was built here in 1820. Little Falmouth produced several ships for the Royal Navy and the Falmouth Packet service during the early 19th Century. Sheila Bird gives details of several notable vessels from later years, including the *Charlotte Padbury*, which when launched in 1874 was said to be the largest barque built in Cornwall. Today, many RNLI lifeboats are serviced here.

FLUSHING

Since at least as far back as the Norman Conquest, the Lords of the Manor in this area have been the Trefusis family. "Trefusis" means "fortified place", presumably a true reflection of the precautions required against seafaring marauders in such an exposed spot; and Trefusis Point was originally chosen by Henry VIII as one of four sites for castles to defend Penryn, Truro and the other ports up-river, but later it was decided that two were adequate. Maps from the late 16th century show a house called "Nankersis" (probably meaning "valley of the reed swamp") south west of Trefusis, and with the growth of Falmouth more dwellings were built there, because it was the best point for a ferry crossing, linking Falmouth with Truro via Mylor, Restronguet Passage and Calenick. About 1660, Francis Trefusis decided to emulate Sir Peter Killigrew's success in creating and promoting Falmouth by hiring Dutch engineers, experts in land drainage and the construction of sea walls, to develop the hamlet of Nankersey into a rival port. The quay walls they built used no mortar, and this broke the force of waves by allowing the water to penetrate; probably that is why the walls have survived in good condition. Many of the attractive, slate-hung houses in the village were built for the Dutchmen. They called their temporary home after the place many of them came from, Vlissingen, and although they didn't stay many years the English version of that name has stuck. Francis's son, Samuel Trefusis, tried to get the Post Office Packet Service transferred from Falmouth to Flushing; he failed (partly, no doubt, because his forebears had supported the Parliamentary cause during the Civil War), but he did bring it about that all officers and crew of Packet ships must live in Flushing, and that brought prosperity and an air of elegance and sophistication for a short time to the village as well as increasing the Trefusis family fortune. By the end of the 18th Century Flushing was becoming a popular holiday resort, partly because of its exceptionally mild climate. It depends quite heavily on tourism now, but traditional occupations like boatbuilding, oyster dredging and fishing are still carried on.

6 Immediately after the stile beside the metal farm gate, take the path on your right, follow round to the left behind the Little Falmouth boatyard (*) and up the slope.

7 Turn right at the road and follow it round through the main street of Flushing (*). Linger on the quay for a while: it affords a fine view of Falmouth harbour and of Flushing's waterside houses. Then continue along the main street. (On the site of the house called Carn-Du was once a silver mine.) Follow the road round to the left out of the village, still skirting the water's edge. (Another magnificent view at the corner; and it's worth turning left just after the corner to visit the Bowling Green, now a small park, which commands an impressive panorama. Notice the small quarry at the corner. It is said that before the present road was built the quarry was open to the sea, and boats could enter to pick up stone.)

8 Where Trefusis Road ends, take the main track straight ahead through the trees and over the cattle-grid on to Trefusis Point. The path now skirts the edge of the low cliff, presenting you with five stiles and plenty of mud at gates. Where the shore curves west towards Mylor at Penarrow Point, notice the obelisk on the beach, inscribed T. B., meaning Truro Boundary. The line from here to Messack Point, near St Just, marks the boundary between Truro and Falmouth Harbours, and every six years the ceremony of beating the bounds takes place, when the Mayor, Corporation and Harbourmaster of Truro visit the obelisks at Penarrow and Messack. After the Restronguet Sailing Club you pass among houses before reaching Mylor Dockyard (*) with its marina for pleasure boats. A small restaurant here, The Ganges, opens during the season, and there is a public phone box.

9 Just past the phone box, go through the gate into Mylor churchyard (*), then up past the church (*), through the lych gate, and take the track on the other side of the road, between a house and a

---

MYLOR DOCKYARD

During the Napoleonic Wars the Admiralty built a dock at Mylor in order to supply provisions to the fleet, since Falmouth was too busy dealing with the Packets. The dock was busy again during the Crimean War. The Ganges restaurant was named after the Naval Training Ship which was berthed nearby from 1866 to 1899. During World War II the yard was used by French resistance fighters, and by U.S. troops at the time of the Normandy landings. It is now leased to Mylor Yacht Harbour Ltd.

MYLOR CHURCH AND CHURCHYARD

Mylor Church has a special place in my affections as the home for many years of a little annual music festival (featuring musicians of the calibre of Roger Norrington) which eventually developed into the Three Spires Festival, based at Truro Cathedral. By the time orchestra, chorus and soloists were packed in, there was little room for an audience in the tiny Norman church, so many stood listening at the open doors on those balmy evenings when summers really were summers.... But in any weather this is an idyllic spot. The graveyard has the tallest ancient cross in Cornwall, though some of its seventeen and a half feet are buried, and also some of the most-quoted gravestone inscriptions in the County. I'll leave you to find for yourself the memorials to Joseph Crapp and Thomas James, along with the graves of numerous shipwreck victims, especially those from the *Queen* transport, wrecked on Trefusis Point, and also the *Ganges* memorial to a distressingly large number of boys who died on the training ship anchored off St Just.

bungalow. Here you get a good view of Mylor Creek. Continue along the road which follows the water's edge (or the mud's edge, if the tide is out).

10 At the crossroads turn right, following the sign to Mylor Bridge.

11 At the main road bear right over the bridge, and soon you are back at the car park. *(If you want to continue walking rather than return to your car, simply take the first right turning beyond the bridge - Trevellan Road - and follow the directions for Walk 3.)*

A SHORTER WALK, OMITTING PENRYN
(Just under six miles)

TO START AT MYLOR *Coming from the main car park, walk or drive over the bridge at the head of the creek and take the first left turning, and then first left again, Church Road. There is usually room to park at the start of this road. Continue along the creekside road for about half a mile, and just as you approach a small inlet (Trelew Creek), take the public footpath on the right. Go through the first farm gate, marked Trelew farm, but just before the second one turn left through a small wooden gate; next go through a larger gate or door, and then a 5-bar gate marked "Footpath". Now follows a very pretty path beside a tiny stream. When you emerge into an open field, keep to the right-hand side. A stile brings you to a road; turn left on it. Go straight on at the crossroads. Immediately after the cattle-grid cross the stile on the right; bear left to another stile, and then keep to the right-hand edge of the field. This brings you to the outskirts of Flushing. Go down the road and turn left at the bottom. Now follow the directions from section 7 to return· to your starting-place.*

TO START AT FLUSHING *If you need to park your car, you may be able to do so on the quay; otherwise, drive on through the village and round the corner on to Trefusis Road; there is usually room to park along there. Now follow the directions from 7 to 9, turning left on to the path just after Trelew Creek, as described above. If you have arrived from Falmouth on the ferry and want a walk, simply turn right from the quay and start with direction 7; you could then do six miles by turning back at Trelew, eight miles by going on to Enys and Penryn, or even twelve miles by linking up with Walk 3.*

WALK 3

MYLOR BRIDGE, GREATWOOD, THE PANDORA AND HALWYN

(About four and a half miles.)

The shorter of our two walks based on Mylor continues the path round the beautiful western shores of Carrick Roads and into the equally lovely Restronguet Creek. Apart from Mylor itself there are no villages on this section, and few houses – just the occasional one standing in enviable (I tried hard to avoid "splendid"!) isolation, and small clusters around Greatwood, Restronguet Weir and Restronguet Passage. Refreshments are available there, at the famous Pandora Inn. There are also shops and the Lemon Arms at Mylor. The walking is easy, apart from a steepish hill after Halwyn; the path is well-walked and should be fairly dry underfoot. The mile-or-so of road walking at the end is rather boring, I'm afraid, so you may prefer to get this over with first by doing the walk in reverse, and practise your skills in reading directions backwards. Alternatively, you could avoid some of the road walking by tacking on Walk 2, making one round walk of over twelve miles: a good day out, but not too exhausting if you're reasonably fit. A suggestion on how to link the two walks is given in italics at the end of the directions.

17

Instructions for driving to Mylor Bridge, and comments on parking there, are given at the start of Walk 2.

1 From the car park, turn right down the main village street, Lemon Hill, for a few yards (notice the small clock tower on the left, a gift from Sir William Lemon), and take the left turning, Trevellan Road. Continue along Mylor Creek, following the sign to Greatwood and Restronguet. Where the road bends left, go straight on along the narrow path, and at the breeze-block wall follow round to the left, entering the field by the metal gate. The path crosses the field, heading back to the creekside.

2 At the two gates, you can continue walking along the field edge, or go along the foreshore, returning to the path at the small inlet. As you reach the end of this small peninsula you pass through a stretch of the path famous for its spring flowers – a riot of primroses, celandines, violets, and especially daffodils. The small quay where there is a seat is known as Greatwood Quay; from here there was once a ferry service to the other side of Mylor Creek.

GREATWOOD HOUSE

This fine old house – once owned, according to Frank Pearce, by one Admiral James, who had Nelson as a guest at one of his birthday dinners – was sadly dilapidated a few years ago, but has been sensitively restored and divided into luxury apartments.

RESTRONGUET CREEK

The name looks French, but derives from the Cornish *ros tron-gos*, "promontory nose-wood", wood on a spur of land. Most of this creek dries out at low tide, as a result of the millions of tons of silt deposited in it by the Carnon River, where tin streaming has been carried out for many centuries. Below the mud is a stratum of gravel rich in alluvial tin, and this has been extensively mined, sometimes using underwater shafts. Plans put forward about ten years ago by Billaton Minerals to dredge the creek for tin met with a very mixed reception from local owners of property and small boats; the plans were shelved, but could be brought to light again if tin prices continue the improvement seen early in 1989. Between 1827 and 1915 a mineral railway ran along the northern side: the horse-drawn wagons took copper ore to the quay at Daniell's Point (named after the Daniell family, mining magnates who built the Mansion House in Truro) and brought back coal for the mines. (Fuller details are in *A View from Carn Marth*.) One industry which does still thrive at the mouth of Restronguet Creek, despite the Bonamia disease, is oyster farming: if you look carefully you will see the sticks used to mark the oyster beds.

3 At the signpost take the road to the right, down to Greatwood
House (✱), and follow the signs to Restronguet. *⟨SHORTER WALK: see
end of directions.⟩* Keep left of the tall fir hedge. After
Restronguet Weir, keep left of the pink (when I was last there!)
cottage and pass in front of the small terrace. You are now at the
point where Restronguet Creek (✱) begins; the promontory opposite,
where a few old cottages can just be seen among much grander
modern homes, is Restronguet Point. A ferry service once operated
between there and Restronguet Passage, where the thatched Pandora
Inn is (✱). The path now brings you down to that.

The Pandora Inn

RESTRONGUET PASSAGE
AND THE PANDORA INN

At least as long ago as the 15th Century, one of the main
roads from Penryn to Truro passed through Restronguet Passage:
"There is a passing boat kept here, it being the Post Road and
by much the nearest cut from Falmouth to Truro and the east"
(Lake's *Parochial History of Cornwall*, quoting a document from
1411). The ferry continued till at least the late 1930s, and
in its latter years a second, smaller boat with low sides was
also in use for the convenience of ladies in long skirts. The
inn, originally called the Passage House Inn, was also a
farmhouse. By 1799 it had been re-named the Ship Inn. The
name "Pandora" was first used for it in the mid-19th Century;
it is said to derive from the ship of that name which was sent
to Tahiti to bring some of the *Bounty* mutineers back to
England. She was wrecked (1791), and her disgraced captain
eventually retired to Cornwall. Perhaps he bought the Ship Inn
and re-named it, but there is no firm evidence of that.

DEVORAN

Nowadays, even small pleasure boats have to pick their moment carefully to get up to Devoran without scraping the bottom, and yet not much over a century ago it was among the most important ports in Cornwall, exporting vast tonnages of copper ore from the Gwennap mines for smelting in South Wales, and importing coal from there and timber from Scandinavia for the bobs of the early beam engines and many other uses in the mines. (It has been claimed that the equivalent of 300 square miles of Norwegian forest was underground in Cornwall in the middle of the 19th Century.) Devoran Quay is a fascinating place to visit; see Walk 5 in *A View from Carn Marth*

PENPOL CREEK

The creek is now surrounded by modern houses and bungalows, along with a few old cottages; a century or more ago it was a very different place, with railway sheds, wharves, coal-heaps, two large smelting houses – one for tin, one for lead – a limekiln and a bone mill operated by the tide. A little light industry remained until recently, in the form of Penpol Boat Yard, where luxury yachts were fitted out; but I understand that this has been bought by Peter de Savary. The boat yard is now closed, but plans for future development of the site have not yet been submitted for approval (April 1989). The old, rusty barges moored there now (April 1989) have in recent years provided shelter for boats laid up during the winter.

CARCLEW

The great house of Carclew, overlooking Restronguet Creek, was built in 1728 for Samuel Kempe, a gentleman from Penryn who had married into the Bonython family, owners of Carclew Barton. In 1749 it was bought, together with its deer park, gardens and plantations covering more than a square mile, by William Lemon, who had made a vast fortune, mainly from the copper mines. (His name is perpetuated in Lemon Street and Lemon Quay, Truro, as well as Lemon Hill and the Lemon Arms at Mylor Bridge.) Carclew House was burnt down in 1934, and little remains except part of the Ionic façade. The splendid gardens, famous for their rhododendrons, lily pond and lake, are occasionally opened to the public: for details, see the annual *Gardens of Cornwall Open Guide*, published by the Cornwall Garden Society.

4 Just past the Pandora, follow the sign to Halwyn. At Restronguet Yacht Basin take the track to the left of the blue-and-white (till it's re-painted) shed. Now you have views along Restronguet Creek towards Devoran (*); Penpol Creek (*) is opposite. After passing the white house at the water's edge, follow the surfaced road up, over three cattle-grids.

5 At Halwyn house, turn left. At the top of the slope there is a fine inland view towards Carn Marth, about five miles away, with an old engine house (Penhale) perched on its side. The farmland and woods in the foreground are mostly the Carclew (*) estates. There is no public right of way through them, so here we have one of only three short stretches between Falmouth and Truro where there is no public footpath or road beside the water. (The others are between Feock and Trelissick, and between another Halwyn, near Old Kea, and Truro.)

6 At the road, turn left, and where the road forks keep right (Bell's Hill). At the first T-junction turn left, and at the second turn right to return to the car park. (*If you would like to do Walk 2 now instead of returning immediately to Mylor, turn right rather than left at point 6, then take the next left turning. Where this road is joined by a slightly busier one from the right, bear left. About a quarter of a mile later, turn right at the first surfaced road (Broads Lane), signposted Elim Cottage. Now follow the directions for Walk 2, starting at point 2.*)

SHORTER WALK, OMITTING THE PANDORA AND HALWYN
(About three miles)

For this, the best place to park, if there's room, would be beside the creek at Mylor Bridge: drive along Trevellan Road, and just past the Post Office is space for several cars. Follow directions 1 and 2, but at the signpost (start of 3) turn left along a quiet country road, as directed for Restronguet Barton. After about a quarter of a mile you have a fine view to the left at the corner, and further glimpses to the right after that. Continue for another half mile. Soon after passing Restronguet Barton you reach a T-junction; here turn left and follow the footpath signposted to Mylor Bridge, which starts on the other side of a metal farm gate. Now simply keep beside the hedge on the left all the way down to the suggested parking place by Mylor Creek.

Restronguet Creek

WALK OUTLINE NO. 1
DEVORAN, POINT, PENPOL AND FEOCK
(About six miles)

Apart from being a very beautiful walk, this is the most interesting to the industrial archaeologist of all walks around the Fal. Among other things, it includes the remains of the quay at what was once one of Cornwall's leading ports; the track of an early mineral railway; and the sites of at least four underwater tin-mines and of two smelting houses. For detailed directions and historical notes, see Walk 5 in *A View from Carn Marth*.

Swans at Pill Creek, Feock

WALK 4

TRELISSICK, COWLANDS, COOMBE AND OLD KEA
*(About eight miles,
but two shorter walks are also suggested.)*

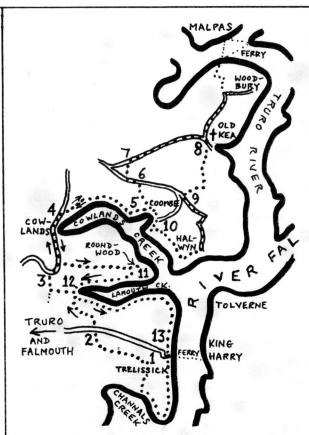

Trelissick makes a good base for a walk, because it provides ample parking (free to National Trust members) and has a shop and restaurant – three things you won't find anywhere else on this route. Trelissick also has (1989) a bus link with Truro, Cornwall Busways Service 85; according to the current timetable, you would need to get out at Four Turnings (Penelewey) and walk from there to Trelissick if you wanted to start the walk in the morning, but you could return direct from Trelissick in the afternoon. The walk itself is very beautiful, offering a great variety of open and wooded countryside plus river and creek views, a ruined church, a pretty waterside village, probably some big ships, and a chance to visit the famous garden and the new arts-and-crafts gallery at Trelissick. Not much road walking is involved, and most of that is on quiet back roads. The paths are usually muddy in places.

To drive to Trelissick from Truro, take the A39 south towards Falmouth, and at the double roundabout (Playing Place) take the second left turning, just beyond the garage; from there follow the signs to King Harry Ferry until you reach Trelissick. Coming from Falmouth, take the first right turning at the Playing Place roundabout.

TRELISSICK

A house was built on this beautiful site about 1750 for a military captain. In 1800 it was bought by R. A. Daniell, nicknamed "Guinea-a-minute" because that was supposed to have been his earnings from Wheal Towan at Porthtowan, only one of several mines he owned. His son Thomas had the house rebuilt on a grander scale with an Ionic portico, and laid out roads through the estate; only six years later he ran out of cash and sold the property to the Earl of Falmouth. Eventually it came into the hands of the Copeland family of the Spode China Factory at Stoke-on-Trent. In 1955 Mrs Copeland presented the house and 376 acres of parkland to the National Trust, but the house is still lived in by the family and is not open to the public. The garden, however, is open every day between 1st March and 31st October (from 11 a.m. except Sundays, 1 p.m.), and the Woodland Walk is open at all times.

Lamouth Creek, still a peaceful and remote-feeling spot despite the popularity of the National Trust's Woodland Walk at Trelissick.

1 The route begins with part of the northern section of the National Trust's Woodland Walk; if you haven't already got the NT's leaflet No. 17, I recommend you buy one (60p, available in the shop at Trelissick). From the car park at Trelissick (*), walk away from the house and garden, crossing a cattle grid and following the road which runs through the park. After crossing a second cattle grid (from which point you may be able to make out a large modern house, Lis Escop, the official residence of the Bishop of Truro, among trees to your left), turn right across the grass towards the lodge.

2 Cross the road (PLEASE BE CAREFUL, because the ferry traffic along this road usually seems to be in a hurry) to the gate opposite, and now follow the Woodland Walk down until you see below you the new wooden bridge over the stream at the head of Lamouth Creek. Go down to it but don't cross it: take the track going left, which follows the course of the stream. *SHORT WALK 1: see end of directions.* After going through the kissing-gate, take the track on the right, over the bridge and up to a road.

3 At the road, turn right, and in less than half a mile you will come to Cowlands....just three or four houses at the head of a tidal creek. Continue over the low bridge.

4 Now you can walk to Coombe (*) along the foreshore if the tide is out (though one part is always soggy, and here a path runs close to the creekside), or continue a few yards up the road and take the woodland footpath on the right. (There is less to see on this route, but it takes you among the orchards for which this area is famous locally....and you could always use the foreshore route later.) After the house, where the path turns left, bear right over a stile; after a second stile turn right. A gate brings you to a house where bric-a-brac is usually on sale; turn right here and then follow the path to the left by the side of the creek.

5 When you reach the end of Coombe Creek, where most of the houses are, take the footpath on the left, signposted Lower Lanner Farm. *SHORT WALK 2: see end of directions.* Where the main track curves left towards Cowlands, go straight on up and over the stile. Now head for the highest part of the ridge in front of you, then go

---

COOMBE

This place is famous locally for its orchards, and in the autumn a very popular Sunday afternoon outing from Truro is to come and buy apples and the small, damson-like Kea plums which are special to this area. At the right season you can pick them for yourself from the low-growing trees along Cowlands Creek.

through the gap in the wall. Still keep to the highest part of the field (good views from up here, of Cowlands and Coombe Creeks behind, the lonely tower of Old Kea church to the right, and a glimpse of Malpas further off). You should now come to a stile; cross it and follow the hedge ahead to another stile (rickety!), which brings you to a road.

6 Turn left, and after a few yards, when you reach Lower Lanner Farm, go through the gate on the right (that is, on the opposite side of the road); here a short path along by the hedge brings you to another stile and another road.

7 Turn right, and continue for about half a mile to Old Kea (*),

OLD KEA

A new parish church of St Kea was built on the western side of the A39 in 1802 when the original 15th Century one, very distant from most of the houses in the parish, fell into disrepair. Now all that remains is the strangely impressive tower, slowly disintegrating. This tranquil place, well known for its jackdaws, is especially lovely in early spring when the churchyard is a mass of snowdrops. The small mission church near the tower is worth a visit. (Incidentally, the 1802 church was itself replaced in 1894.)

The ruined tower is all that is left of Old Kea Church. Below it is Church Creek, sometimes known as Parson's Creek.

where you may be greeted by a herd of goats. The remains of the church are worth a visit; and if you have time and energy to spare (because it's almost a mile there-and-back) it is also pleasant to go down the lane signposted Woodbury Farm (turning left as you arrived at Old Kea). Just before you reach the gate at Woodbury there is a footpath left, down through woodland to the banks of the Truro River opposite Malpas - an unusual view of this attractive village. (There is a ferry connection between here, Malpas and the promontory opposite, where the ferryman's cottage is, but it can operate to and from Woodbury only within an hour or so of high tide.) Return to Old Kea by the same route.

8 Go on down the lane past the church, with Church Creek to your left, through the metal farm gate, and follow the track up. Now head for the second from the left in the line of trees (look back for a pretty view of Old Kea), and then make for the metal gate to the left of the small building. Then turn right and follow the path past the farm buildings to the road.

9 Turn left for Halwyn, then keep left at a farm entrance. (Notice the view of Truro from here.) Lower down, follow the sign to Coombe, and when you get to the ruined farm (Halwyn) keep to the

Sea-going ships laid up in and above King Harry Reach, as seen from Halwyn, March 1989.

TOLVERNE

"Smugglers Cottage", reputedly at least 500 years old, is now a favourite stopping place for pleasure boats plying the Fal. This is an area with many World War II associations: there are relics of concrete slipways and jetties, and even a species of Australian barnacle which probably arrived here on ship bottoms at that time. General Eisenhower is said to have spent time at Tolverne when the D-Day landings were being planned, and it was an embarkation point for US soldiers and tanks on their way to Normandy.

---

right of the buildings. Now go up a few yards to the largest field and walk with the hedge on your left. Fine views of the Fal here, with Tolverne (✱) on the far side. Cross the stile on your left (easily missed!), and this wooded path leads you very attractively down to Coombe. On the way, you get a view of Roundwood Quay (✱), on the far side of Cowlands Creek.

Roundwood Quay. Lamouth Creek is on the left, and the Iron Age fortification is hidden among the trees above the bungalow.

10 Back at the point where the path to Lower Lanner starts (see No. 6), you now have the choice of returning to Cowlands via the foreshore or by paths a bit futher inland – for example, you could follow the Lower Lanner sign and bear left for Cowlands where signposted. At Cowlands, leave by the same road you originally came by, past Penwerris Pottery and Tregew Cottage. At the brow of the hill take the track on your left (no gate), which leads to Roundwood Quay. Go through the gate near the bottom, past the houses and on to the Quay.

ROUNDWOOD QUAY

As far back as the Iron Age the Roundwood promontory was fortified, two ramparts with ditches being built inland and a fort on the hilltop, now shrouded in trees but still obvious. Late in the 18th Century, a substantial granite quay was built, mainly for the shipping of copper ore from the Gwennap mines to South Wales for smelting. Tin was handled, too, and some tin smelting was carried out at Roundwood. Ships of 300 tons could dock here, but on land the transport problem was considerable, with pack-horses churning the unsurfaced roads into a mudbath. With the arrival of the Redruth and Chasewater Railway at Devoran, this quay and the one further south at Pill Creek, Feock, lost their trade from the mines, but coal and lime continued to be delivered at Roundwood, and shipbuilding developed: hence the slipways.

---

11 Until and unless the National Trust create a path direct from the Quay to Trelissick, the easiest route is as follows. Walk back past the houses and up the lane till it curves right where there are two gates on the left. The first gate bears a notice from the NT about parking at Roundwood Quay. Go through this gate and follow the wide track ahead, which gradually curves right and soon brings you through a gap in a wall to an open field. From here on the way is very clear. *A worthwhile short diversion would enable you to see the impressive circular earthwork. Fork left about 20 yards after the gate. Soon you cross the ditch of the outer rampart; just beyond the wooden bench comes the inner rampart. You could continue along the path through the centre of the hill fort, and follow the narrower paths curving right which eventually return you to the wooden bench; from there retrace your steps to the wide track near the gate and turn left.*

12 After crossing the wooden bridge, turn left and follow the Woodland Walk along the other side of the creek and round to King Harry Reach (*).

KING HARRY REACH

Otherwise known as King Harry Passage, this quite narrow channel is remarkable for the depth of water: about 50 feet for much of its width and 80 feet in places - ample for some of the world's biggest ships. Since it is one of the cheapest places in the country to lay up ships that are temporarily redundant, or queuing for a berth at Falmouth Docks, or awaiting their last voyage to the scrapyard, there are sometimes dozens here, manned by skeleton crews. The one-time educational cruise ship, SS *Uganda*, later employed as a hospital ship during the Falklands war, had her last British home here for a few sad months before she went to the Far East to be broken up.

KING HARRY FERRY

In 1988 the King Harry Steam Ferry Company published an interesting booklet in celebration of its centenary. The present ferry, built at Penryn in 1974, is powered by diesel engines, but it still operates by means of chains fixed to either bank. Before 1888, horses, cattle and sheep, as well as people and their carriages, were ferried across in what looks in the old photographs like a tiny, flimsy boat, and according to the booklet, "It was usual for a man to be posted at Turnaware Point, to retrieve boat and tide-swept animals!" There are many tales of liquor-smuggling connected with the ferry. The "King Harry" is usually believed to have been Henry VI: the family who owned the area at the time of his murder in 1471 dedicated a chapel to him and St Mary on the Roseland side. Little trace of it remains.

13 When you come down to the road going to the King Harry Ferry (*), you can return directly to Trelissick by turning right, walking up the hill and eventually entering the grounds via the door beside the turret; but the road is a boring uphill trudge and busy with ferry traffic, so I recommend you to continue the Woodland Walk (up steps opposite the point where you came down to the road) round into Channals Creek and back up the hill to the left of Trelissick House.

A Cross-Channel Ferry laid up in King Harry Reach, as seen from the Woodland Walk, March 1989.

SHORT WALK 1
(About three miles, via Channals Creek)
Instead of turning left by the bridge, turn right, and follow the directions from point 12.

SHORT WALK 2
(A little over six miles, via Channals Creek)
Return to Cowlands direct from Coombe, following the directions from point 10.

WALK OUTLINE NO. 2
TRURO, NEWHAM AND CALENICK
(About four and a half miles,
plus a possible diversion of under a mile)

As another walk of special interest concerning Cornwall's industrial past, this one is also included in *A View from Carn Marth* (as Walk 6). After visiting the docks area of Truro, it follows a former railway track on the south of the city and ends with a short tour of Truro itself. Attention is paid especially to the story of Truro as a port; the history of tin smelting in this area; and the town houses built by the men who made their wealth from mining. The route includes creekside scenery, attractive countryside and a picturesque village.

Truro and the Truro River as seen from Newham

WALK 5

TRURO, ST CLEMENT, TRESILLIAN AND MALPAS

(About seven and a half miles.
If you omit Tresillian, about five miles.
SHORT WALK: about three miles: see end of directions.)

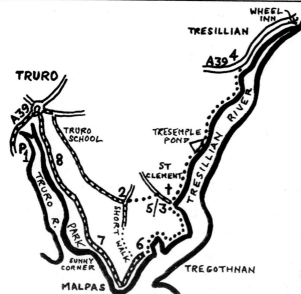

A very pretty walk, mostly beside the waters of the Truro and Tresillian Rivers. St Clement is a charming and peaceful tiny waterside village with a picturesque old church; Malpas is rather larger and busier, at least in summer, when there is much boating activity. It commands fine views over the two rivers. Tresillian is spoilt by the main road, but the walk there from St Clement is lovely, affording good views of the quiet shores of the Tregothnan estate opposite. There is a mile or more of road walking in Malpas and from there to Truro, but all of it is attractive and not normally busy; most of the way there is a pavement or roadside path. Three buses a day (1989) run between Truro and Malpas. There is a very popular pub, the Heron, at Malpas, where you can also find a small shop; the well-known Wheel Inn at Tresillian is unfortunately too far along the A39 to be of much use to you on this walk. The first part of the route is from Truro to St Clement across country, along back roads and lanes and through fields, with occasional glimpses of the water. One section is usually very muddy, so please use suitable footwear. If you walk on from St Clement to Tresillian you have to return by the same path, unless, of course, you take a bus back to Truro from Tresillian.... but it would be a shame to miss Malpas.

The directions are given from the main long-stay car park in Truro, near the big Tesco store beside the main road (A39).

1 Walk to the busy roundabout where St Austell Street meets the A39 (Tregolls Road), take the turning signposted to St Clement (i.e. St Clement's Hill), and almost immediately turn right, up Trennick Lane. This takes you through the grounds of Truro School (*).

TRURO SCHOOL

Truro School is an independent school founded by the Methodist Church in 1880. To quote from David Mudd's *Around the City* (Bossiney Books), "It is almost impossible to believe that Truro School, with its imposing buildings and beautiful site, was bought, built and equipped for a mere £10,000."

Continue up the tarmacked road for about half a mile (notice the view to the right of the Truro River, including the factories and warehouses of Newham), until it bears right at a farm (Trennick). Now take the track which goes on straight ahead, to the left of the buildings. This tends to be muddy, being frequently churned up by farm vehicles, and as it descends to the valley bottom it is crossed by a stream.... Here's the patch you were warned about! The track continues up the other side of the valley – in May it is heavy with the scent (if that's the word) of onion from the "white bluebells" which line it.

2 When you reach the road, turn left and then immediately right. *⟨SHORT WALK: see end of directions.⟩* After the metal 5-bar gate, continue straight ahead, with the hedge on your left at first, and then across the field. If you keep more-or-less to the line of the telegraph cables you will find the stile that brings you back on to the clear path. This takes you past a few buildings; at the road, turn right down the hill into St Clement (*). There are public toilets on the right just before the church (and notice the unusual collection of cups which decorates the old stone shed just beyond the toilets). The church has a slate-hung room over its lych gate. Liz Luck says this "has served as parish vestry room, village school, Sunday school and pigsty." The church itself, with its attendant cottages, tempts every photographer who sees it. Notice the straw birds perched on top of the small thatched roofs of the porches on one cottage.

3 When you get down to the waterside, if you want to limit the walk to about five miles turn right and follow the directions from No. 5; if you want to walk on to Tresillian turn left and keep to the path which follows the edge of the river all the way there. The water on your left at one point is Tresemple Pond, and all the quiet woodland on the far bank is part of the Tregothnan Estate, the seat of the Boscawen family, Lord and Lady Falmouth.

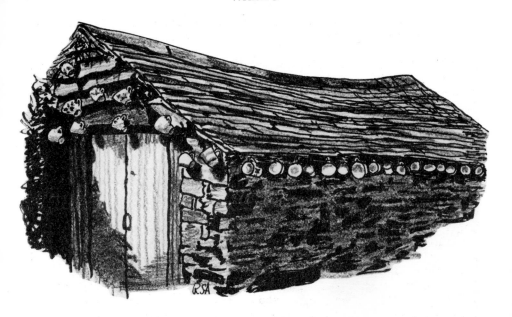

4 The path, after joining a small road for a few yards, brings you out on to the A39 at Tresillian. This hardly makes for pleasant walking, but if you turn right and continue for at least half a mile your efforts will be rewarded by The Wheel Inn (*). If you've had enough walking now, there are plenty of buses to Truro from Tresillian (although of course they are few and far between when you're waiting for one). The intrepid walkers need to return to St Clement by the same waterside path, which leaves the main road just past the bungalow called Rose Neath.

5 At St Clement, continue along the waterside path, here named Denas Road (*). This stretch (which is in fact privately owned, and has only quite recently been made available for public use) is especially attractive, with views towards Tresillian at one end and towards Malpas at the other, and is well endowed with wild flowers, particularly in spring. There are several stiles, one of them a ladder stile which demands some care in crossing. Yellow arrows on wooden posts guide the way, but you can hardly go wrong so long as you keep close to the water. At the head of a small inlet, "Denas Road" joins another path, and you follow it over a plank bridge and into Malpas (*).

6 From here on, it's simply a matter of following the road through the village, past the Heron Inn (opposite which the buses to Truro depart), and on for a further two miles into Truro. Soon after leaving the village, you can avoid walking beside the road by taking the path down by the water's edge. *Directions continue on page 38*

ST CLEMENT

J. B. A. Hockin, in his wonderfully rich and readable book, *Walking in Cornwall* (1936), calls St Clement (actually he says "St Clements") "a tiny unfrequented village in a setting that delights me more than St Just's because it is less posed." He then spoils the effect somewhat by adding, "The church has the

most hideous stained glass I have ever seen." (Is this really the same church John Betjeman described in his *Shell Guide*? ".... with pretty patterned glass inside the windows, red, blue and yellow on a clear ground, which give a twinkling Victorian effect".)Hockin goes on to refer to the well-known inscribed stone (then standing in the vicarage garden, but now near the porch), which "apparently did duty over two separate post-Roman graves before being adapted into a Celtic, wheel-headed cross." It is known as the Ignioc Stone, being dedicated to a 3rd Century Roman, Igniocus Vitalis, son of Torricus. At Yealhampton in Devon is a similar stone dedicated to Ignioc's father. The stone at St Clement is made even more interesting by also having inscriptions in Ogham, a Celtic alphabet normally used only in Ireland. The church dates from the 14th Century (the date 1326 is cut into the tower) but was largely re-built in 1865.A point of interest inside is the Polwhele Aisle, dedicated to Richard Polwhele, a local man who while Vicar of Manaccan near Helford wrote a famous history of Cornwall (1803-8). The St Clement area is rewarding for birdwatchers, and a list of species recently observed is sometimes displayed on a noticeboard near the shore: over sixty were recorded in the first two weeks of April 1988, for example.

THE WHEEL INN, TRESILLIAN

The Inn dates from the 14th Century. In the Civil War it was General Fairfax's headquarters, and it was at Tresillian Bridge that the Cornish Royalists surrendered. On New Year's Eve each year a hundred guests tuck into a huge Cornish pasty, eight stone in weight and six feet long.

DENAS ROAD

This attractive footpath was created by Conservation Volunteers in 1986. Its name, found often elsewhere in forms like Pendennis, means "fort", and here it refers to Moresk Castle, which is believed once to have stood about half way between St Clement and Malpas, where it could guard both the landing place at the former and the ferry-point at the latter. It was apparently destroyed in the 12th Century, during a civil war between King Stephen and his cousin Mathilda. St Clement was part of the ancient Manor of Moresk, which extended as far north as St Erme and included part of Truro; it is an area linked in history and legend with King Mark, Tristan and Isolda: see the note about Malpas.

MALPAS

Usually pronounced "Mopus" or with its first syllable to rhyme with "fall", the name derives from the French "le mal pas", bad step. Oliver Padel comments, "The name is likely to have been given in the 12th century, and suggests that the river here was regularly, though unpleasantly, crossed at that period." Legend tells that, disguised as a leper, Tristan, nephew of King Mark of Cornwall, carried Iseult (Isolda) across the river at Malpas. It's hard to believe, especially as the water was presumably deeper in the 6th Century, silting-up having occurred later. Perhaps one should interpret the tale as evidence of how ancient the triangular ferry service here is. Quite large cargo vessels still pass Malpas occasionally on their way to dock at Newham, Truro, and until recently there was a fuel depot at Malpas, now replaced by bijou residences. The wife of the ferryman, whose pretty cottage is on the headland on the Tregothnan side, told me of her regret at the change: when the ships used to moor there the crews made friends with the family at the cottage, and sometimes at night they were asked to leave their lights on to guide the ships round the bend. She also said that formerly there was a big heronry nearby among the Woodbury trees, but the noise caused by the building work drove the herons down-river. Despite such perhaps regrettable changes, it's obviously not just the excellent food at the Heron Inn that makes so many people flock to Malpas.

Looking down the Truro River at Sunny Corner

7 At Sunny Corner you have to return to the road for a short stretch, but just beyond the Truro Cricket Club ground you can walk through the playing fields and park. (This is Boscawen Park, formerly known as Swan Park.)

8 As you enter Truro you will see commercial wharves on the far bank (*). You can escape some of the ugliness of the last few hundred yards of the road by taking the high footpath on the right, which runs beside an attractive old terrace, and soon returns you to the roundabout and car park.

TRURO

This walk shows quite well what isn't always noticed by visitors: that Truro was once an important port, and still has ambitions in that direction. Fuller details are given in *A View from Carn Marth*, in which Walk 6 explores the Newham shore as well as some of the more interesting parts of the city itself.

SHORT WALK
TRURO AND MALPAS ONLY
(Just over three miles)

At point 2, when you reach the road turn right and continue up the road, which becomes a grassy track at the point where there are three field entrances. This takes you direct to Malpas, with a steep descent into the village. From there, follow the directions from point 6.

WALK 6

RUAN LANIHORNE AND LAMORRAN

(About six miles.
Possible extension of about one mile.
For a shorter walk, see end of directions.
Walks 6 and 7 could be linked,
so the map is at the start of Walk 7.)

Since the early years of the 19th Century, though not today, the upper reaches of the Fal have been used to carry away china clay waste, and thousands of tons must have been deposited at the point where the river met tidal water. This walk starts by crossing the salt marsh created largely by that process. (I have been told that an attempt to mine for tin was made at Foxhole Creek, between Lamorran and Sett Bridge, and the miners found that the depth of the china clay deposit there was 49 feet.) Much of the route is within the vast Tregothnan estate owned by Lord Falmouth; it passes through beautiful woods, open farmland, and then more woods beside a creek where the tiny church of Lamorran nestles among a few pretty houses. The walk is based on Ruan Lanihorne, one of the most attractive and interesting villages around the Fal. The main walk is almost entirely on quiet roads and well-made tracks. A worthwhile short extra is suggested, in the form of a woodland path inland beside the Fal. The only pub on the route is in Ruan, and there is no shop. Telephone boxes are available at Ruan and Lamorran.

To drive to Ruan Lanihorne (*) from Truro, take the A39 eastwards. About a mile past Tresillian, turn right for Tregony, and as soon as you have crossed the bridge over the Fal there, turn right, signposted Ruan Lanihorne. This road runs beside the Fal. From Falmouth the best route is via the King Harry Ferry. After the crossing, drive via Philleigh to Ruan High Lanes, taking the minor road left to Ruan Lanihorne from there.

The King's Head is an attractive pub (rebuilt after being burnt down in 1891), and a deservedly popular eating place. If you intend to be a customer, you could park there; otherwise, there are several places in the village where roadside parking would be unlikely to impede traffic.

1 Go down the narrow road opposite the pub, past the church's lych gate, and turn right at the bottom. Continue on this road beside the tidal Ruan River in its flood-plain, and as you leave the village look back to see a typical small Cornish port with

39

RUAN LANIHORNE

Amazingly, Ruan was once the site of a seven-towered castle, reputedly finer than any other castle in Cornwall save Launceston until early Tudor times. Apparently it was built on the slopes below where the pub now stands. It was erected, probably in the 14th Century, by a family called Archdeacon or Lercedekne, then lords of the manor. According to a note in the church, they died out in the 15th Century; the castle fell into ruins, and local builders pillaged the stone. Sheila Bird, however, states that the castle "was badly damaged in the November gale of 1703." Certainly nothing visible remains now. The signs warning of floods along the lower road are a reminder that even now the tidal waters have not quite deserted this village, which had a period of importance as a port when Tregony became less and less accessible to ships. It is still quite easy to imagine the scene of boats discharging and loading cargoes, both in the village itself and also later at the small Point Quay down-river; ships of 80 to 100 tons sailed up the River Ruan as recently as the early 20th Century. There were winches to haul in bags of coal weighing over 200 lbs for storage in the warehouses beside the quay till the farm carts came for them. After the 1914-18 War, the government sold off army lorries cheaply, and this was another factor, along with the silt, that killed off the river trade. The old, grey church, dedicated like several others in Cornwall to St Rumon, although nothing seems to be known about him, was restored in Victorian times, but, to quote from Liz Luck, "stout, stumpy and rubble-built with ivy and creepers ranging in abandon over the walls, it has an air of dignified dilapidation." Buried near the altar is the Rev. John Whitaker (1735-1808), a prolific author and the writer of a detailed and fascinating *History of Ruan Lanihorne*. H. L. Douch's edition of this is available from the County Museum in Truro - excellent value at £1. The graveyard contains some impressive family tombs, surrounded by railings. All this plus old cottages, a watermill and a pleasant inn.....

tussocky grass instead of waves lapping its harbour. As the road curves right, notice the old quay beside the stream, restored and presented to the parishioners in 1919. Soon comes the delightful Sett Bridge over the River Fal. In Tudor times, Tregony had been an important port; but gradually the silt deepened, and the building of Sett Bridge in 1882-3 (at a cost of £40), and of the weir beside it, finally put an end to navigation up-river. From this point, you can glimpse the stack of the old brickworks near Trelonk: see Walk 7.

Sett Bridge and the River Fal

2 (*Now, or when you return here later, you could make a very attractive short diversion to walk through the woods above the river. If you're lucky enough to be here in May, this is definitely not to be missed, because of the wonderful display of bluebells and wood anemones. Roger Burrows reports that there are wild deer in these woods, probably strays from the large herds at Tregothnan. The path starts on the right side of the bridge as you look inland; where it forks, go either way: both paths end at a barbed-wire fence, and you have to return to Sett Bridge by the same route.*)

Now the road goes curving up into the woods, with high, mossy, flower-covered banks.

3 At the sharp left bend, turn right on to the track marked Unsuitable for Motors. ⟨*SHORT WALK: see end of directions.*⟩ The track climbs out of the woods and then runs beside a wire fence.

LAMORRAN

Apart from some restoration work in the 19th Century by members of the Boscawen family of Tregothnan, the little 13th century church of St Moran (who was female - but that's all we know) and the surrounding buildings have been protected from modern improvements. John Betjeman complained, in his *Cornwall: A Shell Guide*, that the church was usually locked and "the key kept over a mile away", but he obviously managed to gain access, and gives a description of the oil-lit interior. The oak woods once provided an income for the few local people: the timber was used for ship-building and the bark for leather tanning. (The old tannery at Grampound, higher up the Fal, still operates.)

Go through the right-hand gate. A second gate brings you to Gare Farm; you pass between the farm buildings and the mansion. The footpath shown on the O.S. maps as going left from here is unfortunately blocked, so continue along the road, and bear left at the T-junction towards Lamorran and Ruan, as directed by the old signpost – one of the prettiest I've seen in Cornwall. There follows about a mile of pleasant, level walking on a quiet road with extensive views over the Roseland countryside. Ignore the right turning to Tresillian.

4   At Tregenna Farm turn right. After Trewonnal Farm you descend into the wooded valley.

5   Turn left for Lamorran at the T-junction. Here the woods have been thinned a good deal lately, perhaps because of elm disease. Soon you are walking by a stream, and this gradually opens out into a pool created by a sluice gate at Lamorran (*). The pool, once the site of a duck decoy, is one of the few places in Cornwall where moorhens breed. The church at the sharp left bend in Lamorran is worth inspecting, but it's likely to be locked. There is an ancient cross in the graveyard. Continue past the beautiful Old Rectory and a small quarry. Now the road winds uphill among bulbfields which are a fine sight in early spring. Turn right at the sign to Ruan Lanihorne, and soon you are back at Sett Bridge; return to your car by the same route as at the start – except that in the village you could either take the first left turn, or – best of all – continue along the bottom road to see the old warehouses and other buildings dating from Ruan's period as a port. Turn back sharp left for the pub and church.

SHORT WALK, OMITTING GARE
(About four and a half miles)
At point 2, ignore the track and continue on the road. Turn right at the T-junction, and go on for almost a mile to Tregenna, rejoining the longer walk route at point 3, where you turn left.

WALK 7

RUAN LANIHORNE, TRELONK, TRENESTRALL AND TREWORGA

(About four miles.
Possible extension of about two miles.
See end of directions for shorter walk.
Walks 6 and 7 could be linked.)

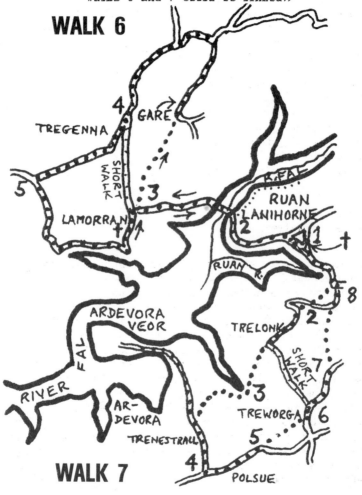

For directions to Ruan Lanihorne and comments on parking, see Walk 6.

1 From the church, walk past the King's Head. Soon you reach Ruan Mill, where the former position of the waterwheel can easily be deduced from the course of the old leat. Notice the bell on the top of the white house a short way beyond: this was once the village school. Opposite Tregellas, take the path signposted on

A gentle, easy walk through very remote-feeling countryside with occasional glimpses of the river. There are few trees, in great contrast to the other recommended walk from Ruan Lanihorne. The suggested extension to Ardevora Veor should not be missed, because the view from this remote spot is exceptional, even by the usual standards of the Fal area. Most of the route is on minor roads or well-made tracks, but there are some paths across fields which are likely to be wet and muddy. Two stiles just after Treworga would be difficult for the less agile walker to manage. There is no shop on this walk, and the only pub is at Ruan Lanihorne. Treworga has a phone box.

the left side of an old building which was till quite recently a blacksmith's shop: notice the horseshoe on the door. The right of way, though not obvious, goes straight up the field: make for the dip on the skyline – and don't miss the lovely view behind, up a valley. (The extent to which the landscape has changed over the centuries is shown by the fact that seashells have been dug up in this valley.) At the top of the slope, near some bungalows and Trethella Farm, go through the wooden gate, beside another public footpath sign, and down some steps.

2 Turn right on the road. After about 200 yards, a footpath on the left cuts off a corner, but it's rather soggy and overgrown with nettles, so you may prefer to continue up the road, which bends sharply left. Continue uphill to the large group of farm buildings at Trelonk (*)   ⟨*SHORT WALK: see end of directions.*⟩   After the farm, where the road bends left, go straight on down the track to a footbridge at the marshy head of Tuckingmill Creek (*).

3 Follow the track round to the right. Go through the metal farm gate as you approach Trenestrall Farm; turn left at the road. *(But I strongly recommend you to turn right for a diversion – about a mile each way if you go as far as the farm buildings– to Ardevora Veor (*); after about half a mile of narrow road with high banks you suddenly emerge at open fields with a truly memorable panoramic view including Ardevora and Ardevora Veor farms, Lamorran on the far side of the river, and the Trelonk brickworks*

TRELONK

Whitaker's *History of Ruan Lanihorne* mentions a tradition that "there was a city at Trelonk formerly, and that a King resided in it." The city stretched as far as Reskivers, near Tregony. There is at least a grain of truth in this, because in the middle ages there was a village called Sheepstall or Sheepstors between Tregony and Ruan. Whitaker believed that *Trelonk* meant "Long House", and for him this confirmed that it was originally the seat of a Baron; modern Cornish studies, however, explain the name as "farm by the gorge or gully". Over the brow of the hill, close to the water, is the tall, square, elegant stack of what was once Trelonk Brickworks. To maintain access to the quay at Ruan, the silt, rich in china-clay waste, was constantly dredged, and some of it was baked in kilns at Trelonk to make the bricks of which many nearby farms are built. According to Sheila Bird, silt was also taken to Penryn in wicker baskets to be turned into concrete blocks. A hide for birdwatching at Trelonk has been constructed by the RSPB and the Cornwall Birdwatching and Preservation Society; a key is available to Society members. For details, write to Mr G. Jackson, Curgurrell Corner, Curgurrell, Portscatho, Truro. For details of the nature reserves here and at Ardevora, contact the Cornwall Trust for Nature Conservation's Warden, Mr S. Gay, Lower Trewithian Farm, Portscatho (Truro 58518).

TUCKINGMILL CREEK

There are several Cornish places called Tuckingmill. "Tucking" is the same as "fulling": cleaning new woollen cloth of grease by scouring, beating and using fuller's earth.

stack further right. Return the same way.) At Trenestrall you pass various interesting farm buildings and houses, and finally you reach what counts in this remote-feeling area as a main road.

4 Turn left. Soon you pass the drive to the Polsue Manor Hotel; then the road descends into a valley.

Ardevora and Ardevora Veor, with Lamorran on the other side of the Fal. The Trelonk brickworks stack is further right – not quite visible from this spot.

ARDEVORA AND ARDEVORA VEOR

A beautiful and remote spot, famous for its birdlife, which includes overwintering spotted redshanks, plus ring plovers and the occasional osprey, spoonbill and avocet. More common are black tailed godwits, golden plovers, dunlin, teal and shelduck, the last of which sometimes nest in rabbit burrows. (The name *Ardevora*, pronounced with the stress on the first and third syllables, means "beside the waters".... Compare Devoran, "waters" — a place where three streams meet. *Veor* means "great".)

5 Just after crossing the stream, take the footpath signposted on the left at the point where the road curves right. You now enter what in April 1989 was a bulbfield; the footpath had been ploughed up and not re-instated. *(If the field is too muddy for comfortable walking, you could keep to the road instead and take the first left turning, rejoining the suggested route at point 6.)* The right of way goes up the field towards the right, gradually diverging from the field-edge alongside the road. When you are high enough to see farm buildings ahead, go just to the right of them, where there is a stile giving on to the road. (From here there is a view of the Fal, with a glimpse of the top of the brickworks stack at Trelonk.) Turn left on the road.

6 Continue along the road through the attractive hamlet of Treworga, bearing right by the phone box.　　Next comes a very pretty stretch, down into another valley.

7 At the bottom, after two driveways on the left, the road bends right; here you cross a rather awkward stone stile on the left, beside a footpath sign to Ruan Lanihorne. Now walk just to the right of straight ahead and cross a tiny stream (probably non-existent in a good summer) to another awkward, broken-down stile. Continue in the same line to the next stile, beyond which is a low wire fence (not barbed). Step over that and walk with the hedge on your right; after the gap, it's on your left. Go through the gateway and still continue straight ahead, cutting off the field corner to join the track where it bends left.

8 After the five-bar gate, ignore the track on the right, but turn right on the surfaced road. At the T-junction turn left, and this brings you back to your starting point.

SHORT WALK, OMITTING TRENESTRALL
(About three miles)
Continue on the road as it bends left after Trelonk farm. This takes you to Treworga, where you turn left and follow the directions from point 6.

WALK 8

ST JUST AND ST MAWES
*(Between five and a half
and seven and a half miles: see below.
Two shorter walks are suggested
at the end of the directions.)*

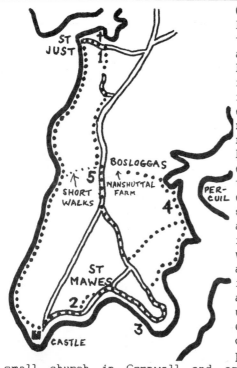

Of all the walks around the Fal that I know, I think this one most nearly approaches my notion of The Perfect Walk..... or rather, it would do, but for one irritating fly in the ointment, and there is reason to hope that that may one day be removed. Details are given in part 4 of the directions; suffice it to say here that the right of way through one very short section is in dispute, and until/unless the matter is resolved in favour of walkers, a longer and less attractive alternative route, involving some walking along a busy road, will have to be used. Whatever the eventual outcome, this remains a delightful walk, starting at probably the most famous small church in Cornwall and continuing along the eastern shore of Carrick Roads; you then have a chance to look over St Mawes Castle before visiting St Mawes (very conveniently placed for "facilities" and refreshments); next comes lovely creek scenery; and finally a ridgetop path with probably the most spectacular views to be had anywhere around the Fal – and that's a big claim to make. If the weather is right for bathing, there are several suitable beaches along the way, some of which are likely to be deserted except perhaps at the very height of the season. Some parts of the path will be muddy in wet periods; there are a large number of stiles to cross and a few hills to climb, but nothing frightening.

There is a convenient free car park at St Just-in-Roseland Church (*). (Directions to King Harry Ferry from Truro and Falmouth are given at the start of Walk 9. Once you have crossed into the Roseland (*), follow signs to St Mawes, and when you reach St Just watch for the right turning to the church.)

1 From the church take the path to the left, close to the creekside. You might care to go down to the foreshore below the path and walk to the right among the boats out on to St Just Bar, where you have a good view of the narrow entrance to St Just Pool and of St Just Creek to the left. After Pasco's boatyard, keep right, following the sign to St Mawes, and bear left at Bar Point house. The path goes to the left of a bungalow. Cross the stile and from there the path keeps close to the edge of the low cliff all the way to St Mawes, giving fine views of Carrick Roads (*). Occasionally a gate or stile by the edge of the low cliff gives you a chance to go down on to the foreshore, where you could walk along the sand and do a little rock-scrambling, if the tide is low enough, as a change from the upper path. *⟨SHORT WALK 1: see end of directions.⟩* Eventually, a gate brings you on to a road at the edge of St Mawes (*), and now you have your first good view of Falmouth Bay to the right and St Anthony Lighthouse to the left. In front is St Mawes Castle (*). After passing this, follow the road into the village.

2 *(At the point where a path to the right leads down to Tavern Beach, you could take the narrow path upwards to the left into Riviera Gardens. These are small but attractive. On leaving them, continue along Riviera Lane and then turn right, past the church and back to the seafront.)* Follow the waterside road right

ST JUST-IN-ROSELAND

Whether you find St Just Church an inspiring place perhaps depends on whether you agree that
    "You are nearer God's heart in a garden
    Than anywhere else on earth."
Each time I go I prepare myself to be repelled by the element of *kitsch* in and around the famous graveyard, with its carefully directed streams, rather twee carved quotations, and every inch beautified by the gardeners (John Betjeman's verdict is: "It is the ideal resting place for lovers of 'Forest Lawn' in America and Woking in Surrey"); but each time I am bowled over by the sheer magic of the setting and the simple charm of the church itself, tucked down so low by the water that from the top of the churchyard you look down on the top of the tower. The building dates from the 13th Century and was restored during the 19th by the architect who also redesigned St Anthony Church, and who seems to have been more sensitive to the spirit of the original buildings than many of his contemporaries were.

ROSELAND

As the map-maker John Norden wrote in 1584; "The peninsula is called by the pretty name of 'Roseland' which has, however, nothing to do with flowers, being derived from 'Rhos', the Celtic word for heath or gorse." Explanations of Cornish place-names are often controversial, though, and you may prefer another scholar's interpretation of 'ros' as 'a point extending into the sea'. In any case, gorse is usually in bloom, so even "heathland" does have something to do with flowers!

CARRICK ROADS

This is the deep-water anchorage for Falmouth Harbour and Docks and towns up-river such as Penryn and Truro. It is said to be the world's third largest natural harbour, after Sydney and Rio de Janeiro. "Rode" would be a more logical spelling, because the word refers to the ability of ships to ride out storms here, or simply to ride at anchor. The water depth varies greatly, from about four feet at low tide north of Mylor to about a hundred feet at the seaward end. The word "Carrick" derives from *garrak*, rock, and refers to Black Rock at the entrance to the Roads; this was previously called *an garrak ruen*, Seal Rock.

ST MAWES
AND ST MAWES CASTLE

Prehistoric remains suggest that there was a settlement and fortress here in pre-Christian times, and that tin was exported from St Mawes in the Bronze Age. The village is named after St Mauditus, a 5th Century Breton or Irish religious teacher. The castle, unusually designed in the form of a clover-leaf as seen from above, dates from 1543, and is one of three Henry VIII planned to build to guard Carrick Roads, Penryn, Truro and Tregony: see the notes on Pendennis Castle (Walk 1) and Flushing (Walk 2). Attack from the landward side was never expected, so during the Civil War its Royalist governor capitulated immediately when Fairfax threatened it in March 1646. In 1562 St Mawes was given the right to elect two MPs – "more by favour than by merit", remarked Richard Carew (1555-1620) in his *Survey of Cornwall* – so it was one of the notorious "Rotten Boroughs" which were disenfranchised in 1832. Not much is left now of the old fishing village: St Mawes became one of Cornwall's most fashionable small resorts early this century, and most of the waterfront area was transformed as a result.

through the village, past the Idle Rocks Hotel. Notice the mesembryanthemums (Livingstone daisies) growing on the small cliff just after the hotel.

3 Just before a group of pine trees there is a path down to the beach. If the tide is low enough you could take this and walk round Polvarth Point on the foreshore, so long as you don't mind scrambling over rocks and stepping over mooring ropes. Continue past the St Mawes Sailing Club, and when you reach a boatyard turn left and follow the footpath signposted "Porthcuel Creek". (Or, if you keep to the road past the pine trees, take the lane on your right just before Freshwater Lane; the footpath to Porthcuel Creek is on the left at the bottom.) The path turns left behind another boatyard; turn right at the lane, down among the boats, and then continue along the waterside again. When you enter a field, keep to the hedge on your right at first, and then cut across the field past a tree with a broken footpath sign beneath it. The path goes on uphill, to the left of several trees. Follow the sign down the steepish path to the right, ignore the stile ahead, and go round to the left behind a wooden building. You are now opposite Percuil (see Walk 9), at the point where there was once a ferry service.

4 *(From here the public footpath continues according to the O.S. maps, but the landowner clearly has other ideas. When I was last there – May 1989 – it was easy enough to cross the low wire fence by the tumbledown wall, and the few hundred yards that follow are among the loveliest bits of the whole walk. Keep by the field-edge*

on the right at first. At the little inlet at Bosloggas, further attempts are made to discourage walkers, but if you can squeeze through between close-set posts at the far end of the tree-trunk you can follow the Public Footpath signs up the pretty valley, walking between two tiny streams and alongside a large woodland garden. After crossing a footbridge and going up two short flights of steps, you will - unless things have changed by the time you get there - be confronted by a "Polite Notice" declaring "No through access" and warning that the public footpath ends soon. Sure enough, a little further on, at Nanshuttal Farm, there is a gate marked "Private - No access" - at which point you have little option but to retrace your steps. The Footpaths Officer for the Carrick region tells me (May 1989) that the dispute may soon be resolved in court, and that he has good hopes of a successful outcome from the point of view of walkers. If that comes about, the route from the farm gate is very obvious, through the farmyard and along the farm drive; it emerges at the road almost opposite the water tower referred to at the start of point 5.) If you do have to go back, return to the top of the "steepish path" (see above) and turn right, passing through a kissing gate. The official path crosses the centre of the field, but by keeping to the hedges on the left you can avoid damaging crops and get a good view over St Mawes as your reward. When you reach some granite

St Just-in-Roseland Church

steps into the next field, cross them and follow straight on, keeping the hedge to your right. (If you look back, you will see that the road from Percuil on the other side of the creek follows in a straight line from the path you're on. In "the old days" this was the usual route from St Mawes to the Percuil ferry.) Another kissing gate brings you to houses; turn left and bear left again, then right on to the main road - rather busy, I'm afraid.

5 After about half a mile, just after the water tower, cross the stile on the left, following the sign to St Just. The path, very recently (1989) created by the National Trust, keeps beside the field edge on the right, close to the road, and includes several fine new stiles. The view along here is breathtaking, and every few yards of walking seem to reveal new aspects of it. Eventually you reach a lane, where you follow the sign to the left. The lane becomes a track and finally a path, rather churned up by the cattle of Churchtown Farm. After passing among a few houses, you reach the road opposite the church's upper lychgate, and from here it is pleasant to walk back to the car park through the Memorial Gardens on the right, rather than along the road. Alternatively, go down to the church again, and then it's worth stepping over the cattle grid in the lower lychgate on the right and strolling a little way along the path beside the creek, which gives you lovely views of the church.

SHORT WALK 1, OMITTING ST MAWES
(About two and a half miles)
This involves quite a steep climb on a path which is usually rather overgrown, with a generous supply of nettles, so wear stout trousers. Just before a stile about a mile south of St Just, follow the sign, "Public Bridleway, St Mawes Garage". About 20 yards after turning left, go right up a grassy track, then immediately left, following the red arrow on a post. This narrow path reaches the road close to a water tower. Cross the stile on the left and continue the directions from point 5.

SHORT WALK 2, OMITTING ST JUST
(Just under four miles, if route through Nanshuttal Farm is open.)
This, too, involves walking on the be-nettled path, but this time downhill. Starting at the main car park in St Mawes, turn left at the sea-front, go past the Idle Rocks Hotel, and then follow the directions from point 3. At point 5, go down the bridleway instead of crossing the stile. You could walk by the field-edge at first, but when this curves left you need to get on to the rather overgrown path. Turn left at the bottom to return to St Mawes.

PORTH, PORTSCATHO AND PERCUIL
(Nearly six miles.
Walks 9 and 10 could be combined,
so the map is on a later page.)

The last two walks, like the first, include some sea coast in contrast to river and creek. This one begins with a gentle section of the South Cornwall Coastal Footpath which has extensive views across Gerrans Bay to the Dodman; next comes an attractive fishing village, with its mother church a little way inland and on top of a hill at Gerrans (quite similar to Gorran Churchtown in relation to Gorran Haven – which is just one of the two reasons why I tend to confuse Gerrans and Gorran!). After the short inland walk come peaceful, secluded creeks, skirted for the most part by a well-made path quite recently provided by the National Trust, although there is one short section near the end that is sometimes rather overgrown, and bare legs might not make for comfortable walking there. There is little road walking involved, and mud is not usually too much of a problem on the paths. Portscatho has shops, a good pub and other facilities, conveniently placed at about the half-way point. There are also toilets at Porth, where the walk starts and ends.

Park at the National Trust car park at Porth Farm (Grid Reference: SW 868329). (To get there from Truro or Falmouth, take the A39 as far as the Playing Place roundabout, which is between Truro and Carnon Downs. Follow signs from there to King Harry Ferry. Except at very busy times, when it tends to set off as soon as it is full, the ferry operates every half hour, apart from Sundays in winter: it leaves on the hour and half-hour from the near (Trelissick) side, and at a quarter to and quarter past the hour from the Philleigh side. After the crossing, follow signs to St Mawes at first. In about a mile, take the left turn, following signs to Gerrans. At Gerrans take the road signposted Anthony Head. About a mile later you pass the head of a creek on your right, and the car park is on your right soon after that.)

1 Take the path marked "Beach" opposite the car park entrance. (Toilets are in the building you pass through here.) The coast path heading towards Portscatho goes off to the left just before you reach the beach (Towan). It is clearly marked all the way to the village. Once you have passed Greeb Point you have good views of Gerrans Bay, with Carne Beacon and Pendower Beach prominent to

the left of Nare Head, and Gull Rock (one of many so named: "Nine, to be precise," says Peter Gilson) off to the right. The church spire is that of Gerrans (*). Soon after entering Portscatho (*) you pass the little Post Office on your right, and then the pub (The Plume of Feathers) before reaching The Square with its various shops.

2 To continue the walk, return to the Post Office and take the footpath opposite, signposted Percuil.

3 At the top of the steep slope and steps, the path goes almost straight on (just slightly right). Make for the corner of a field surrounded by hedges on the left, and then still continue in a straight line till you reach a metal 7-bar gate. This brings you to a lane and soon to a road.

4 Turn left, and soon right over a stile, signposted to Percuil. Now head for the nearest telegraph pole and then to the stile in the wall, going straight on across the next field to another stile which brings you out on to another road. Continue along the path opposite, marked Portcuil.

GERRANS

The name is pronounced with a hard G, and is apparently derived from "St Gerent" or "Geraint" or "Gerennins", King of Cornwall from 580 to 586 A.D. The church, with its un-Cornish-looking spire, dates only from 1849, as the 14th Century church was destroyed by fire.

PORTSCATHO

The name is from Cornish: "landing-place of boats". The locals say it as "P'scatha" or just "Scatha". Farming has always been the main source of income - though the holiday trade may have overtaken it by now - but the pilchard fishery used to be very important. David Mudd, in "Around and About the Roseland" (Bossiney Books, 1980), writes, "The best way of handling heavy landings was to stack them, alternately, head beside tail, with salt between the layers to form a wall of fish several feet high. The weight of fish would cause the simultaneous bursting of air bladders, row-by-row, creating a loud identifiable sound midway between a sob and a sigh. As soon as the air bladders had exploded, the bulk of the fish shrank and there was room for more"...so the pilchards were said to be "crying for more". Luckily, modern visitors are unlikely to be troubled by the stinking, oily scum which used to form stagnant puddles in the streets and pollute the village's water supply.

PERCUIL

The name, probably meaning "the narrow harbour", is pronounced with the stress on the middle syllable: P'cuil, or even as two syllables: P'cule. Variant spellings include Porthcuel, Portcuil and many more. Percuil is now a centre for pleasure boats with a small trade in oysters and lobsters, but till well into this century it was an important trading-port: lime (converted into quicklime by a kiln on the beach) and South American guano for fertilizer were brought by small boats, and coal by bigger ones. Up to 1939 a steam ferry operated between here and Falmouth, and till about 1948 a rowing-boat ferry provided a link with St Mawes.

FROE

The largest house at Froe was once the mill: there was a tide-mill here (as at Polingey, whose name is a variant of Melingey, meaning "Mill pool"), and the pool is clearly separated from the creek by a causeway. Until the early 20th Century, Froe was quite a busy little port: small boats brought in coal and collected grain from the mill. Froe Creek almost makes an island of St Anthony parish, and the neck of land is so narrow here that in storms sea-spray can sometimes be felt at Froe.

roe Creek on a rainy day in May 1988

5 Just past the farm (Tregassick), take the path on your right, marked "National Trust - Footpath to Percuil 1m". Next turn right down the path signposted Polingey Creek. Go through the gate on to a grassy path (with a fine show of campion in May); just before the next gate, cross the stile on the left, go along the right side of the field, and then follow the yellow arrow to the right, over two stiles and down a steep path to Polingey Creek.

6 Turn left (Take care! Badgers have been at work.) and follow the footpath beside the water (or mud, if the tide's out) around to Percuil (*). From the car park, it's worth turning right to look at the boatyard at the former ferry crossing; then return up the road past the car park. A few yards past the car park entrance, cross the stile on the right, signposted Pelyn Creek and Trewince (Cornish: "homestead in the wind") Avenue. From the bench as you approach the creek you have a view south-west along the Percuil River to the outskirts of St Mawes.

7 At the head of Pelyn Creek you have to turn inland. First follow the sign right to Trewince Avenue, cross the stream and the stile to the left, then walk up by the field edge on your left. At Pelyn farm the signposts may be confusing. Cross the stile on the left by the house and then go up the path on the right where there is a gap in the metal fence. (It is marked "Footpath" but was very overgrown when I last walked it....Stout trousers advisable! But you are soon out in the open again.) Cross the stile on to the track and turn left (signed Trewince Avenue) at the farm.

8 At the road, go straight on. Soon you pass Froe Creek (*) and come back to the car park at Porth Farm. You can avoid walking on the road for these last few hundred yards by taking the pretty footpath on the right.

PORTH AND ST ANTHONY IN ROSELAND
(Nearly six miles - or a version about half that length
starting at St Anthony Head. See end of directions.
Walks 9 and 10 could be combined.)

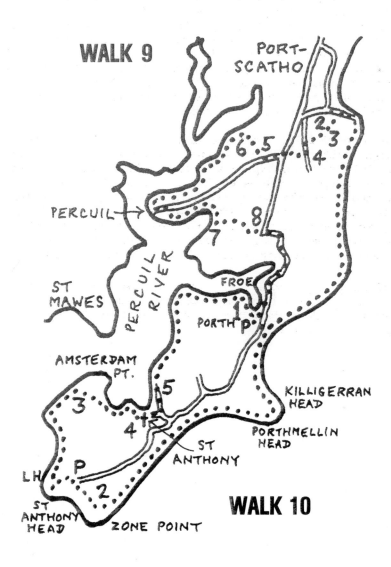

Yet another walk of great beauty and variety, including not only lush creekside settings and panoramic views of Falmouth Harbour and St Mawes, but also some rocky cliffs – hardly spectacular, perhaps, but a dramatic contrast to the soft riverside slopes which in places are only a few hundred yards away across the peninsula. You also pass a large country house in a superb setting, an interesting little church, and a lighthouse which is often open for visits. The path is well marked most of the way and is not usually very muddy. Toilets are available at both Porth and St Anthony Head, but there is no pub, café or shop anywhere along the route, the nearest ones being at Gerrans and Portscatho.

For the longer walk, park at the National Trust Car Park at Porth Farm. (Directions to Porth are given for Walk 9.)

1 Take the path marked "Beach" opposite the car park entrance. (Toilets are in the building you pass through here.) Just before reaching Towan Beach, go up the path on your right on to the cliff. The Coast Path is very clear all the way round from here past Killigerran Head, Porthmellin Head, Porthbeor Beach and Zone Point to St Anthony Head. Less than half a mile after Porthbeor (pronounced "Polbare") you get your first glimpse, over the ridge, of St Mawes, Falmouth Docks and Pendennis Castle, with Place Barton farm in the foreground. As you reach the headland your view also extends along the coast westward to The Manacles (*).

2 As you approach the Head, you pass through the remains of World War I encampments and World War II fortifications; soon afterwards,

ST ANTHONY LIGHTHOUSE AND THE MANACLES

The lighthouse was built in 1835. It is now fully automated, and is run by a man-and-wife team, so opening times for visits cannot be regular, but you may well be lucky. Its light, supplied by a 1500-watt bulb, is visible for 14 miles in clear weather; it shines red in the direction of the Manacles. This is a notorious group of submerged and half-submerged rocks about half way between Falmouth and Lizard Point: the reef stretches a mile and a half out to sea and is two miles wide. The Manacles have been the cause of many a wreck, probably the best-known of which was that of the *Mohegan* in 1898. Their name means Church Rocks (*Maen eglos*): the church spire at St Keverne has traditionally been used as a landmark to help sailors to avoid them.

be careful not to miss the path down to the left, marked "To the Lighthouse". Go down here, and after looking at St Anthony Lighthouse (*), continue along the path which follows the coastline, at the foot of the steps by which you descended to the lighthouse.

As you approach the patch of woodland at Amsterdam Point, you have to turn right and climb the hill. Cross the wall where the granite steps are, and follow the path straight down towards Place House (*). The path takes you round behind it, to the right.

PLACE HOUSE

This stands on the site of a tiny Augustinian priory, built by the monks of Plympton in the 12th Century. When the monasteries were dissolved, about 1536-9, the stones from Place priory were taken by barge to St Mawes as building material for the new castle. Soon after, a large house was built here, bought by the Vyvyan family in Elizabeth I's reign and by the Spry family in the mid 17th Century. Little or nothing of the old house survived the Victorian rebuilding ("symmetrical Neo-Gothic at its least attractive" in the opinion of Nikolaus Pevsner). During World War II it was commandeered by the Royal Navy, and in the immediate post-war years it was a home for displaced Europeans. In 1949 it was converted into a holiday camp; later it became Place Manor Hotel; and since 1982 it has reverted to its old status as a private house, still the home of the Sprys.

Take the path on the left down to St Anthony Church (*). (There is an acorn sign at the turning, but it may be hidden by tall nettles.) After passing the church, go on till you reach a road, and then turn left, past the tiny Place Shellfish Purification Plant.

ST ANTHONY CHURCH

Apparently a Saxon church stood here originally. When the priory was dissolved, the nave of the 12th Century church was spared because it had been in use for public worship. In the 19th Century, soon after Place House was rebuilt, the chancel was rebuilt to match as closely as possible the medieval one, and a tower was added to imitate the one on the house. The South doorway is genuine Norman, as are the tower arches. Despite the high proportion of Victorian work, Pevsner calls St Anthony Cornwall's best example of what churches must have been like in the 12th Century.

5 There is a stile on the right opposite the curved sea wall in front of Place House; cross this and go left, following the sign to Porth Farm. You now enter perhaps the prettiest stretch of the whole walk, with woodland, open fields, fine views back to St Mawes and Pendennis Castles and ahead to Percuil, Porth Creek and Froe.

Cross the footbridge at Froe and take the grassy path on your right, which leads back to the car park.

SHORT WALK
(About three miles)

Park at St Anthony Head, then follow directions 2, 3 and 4 above, but turn right at the road after St Anthony Church. Keep on along the road for about half a mile, ignoring the right turn to Anthony Head, and take the path on the right down to the Coast Path above Porthbeor Beach.

Looking back towards St Anthony Head

FURTHER READING

Roger Burrows: Wildlife of the Fal Estuary (Harbour Books, 1984)

Frank Pearce: Along the Fal (Cornwall County Publishers, no date)

Sheila Bird: Around the Waterways of the Fal (Bird of Freedom, 1988)

Heron

History Around the Fal (five books by the Fal History Group, published by the University of Exeter)

Liz Luck: South Cornish Harbours (Nautical Books, 1988)

David Mudd: Around and About the Fal (Bossiney Books, 1989)

FALMOUTH: Look at the Falmouth Waterfront (Falmouth Civic Society, Marina Press - no date)

Falmouth Town Trail Walkabout (Cornwall Heritage Project, 1986)

Bob Dunstan: Falmouth's Famous Past (Falmouth Packet, 1968)

James Whetter: The History of Falmouth (Dyllansow Truran, 1981)

David Mudd: Home Along Falmouth & Penryn (Bossiney Books, 1980)

Fisher Barham: Old Cornwall in Camera: Falmouth (Glasney Press, 1977)

Peter Gilson: Falmouth in Old Photographs (Alan Sutton, 1990)

PENRYN: Penryn Walkabout (1988 version; an older one is also still available from Ryall's the newsagents.)

James Whetter: The History of Glasney College (Tabb House, 1988)

Rita T. Pope (ed.): Memories of Old Penryn (Dyllansow Truran, 1983)

Shag

Roland J. Roddis: Penryn - The History of an Ancient Cornish Borough (Bradford Barton, 1964)

TRURO: Truro City Centre Walkabout (Cornwall Heritage Project)

Christine Oates: The Truro City Trail (Truran, 1984)

Sheila Bird: Bygone Truro (Phillimore, 1986) (old photographs)

David Mudd: About the City (Bossiney Books, 1979)

June Palmer: Truro in the Seventeenth Century (1989) and Truro in the Eighteenth Century (1990) (Old Smithy Press)

(My own *The Landfall Book of Truro* (1990) includes a city-centre walk with brief historical notes.)

ROSELAND: Laurence O' Toole: The Roseland - between River and Sea Lodenek Press, 1978)

(Most of the above were still in print when I was writing my own contributions, and they should all be in the local libraries, together with Bob Dunstan's *The Book of Falmouth and Penryn* and Leslie Douch's *The Book of Truro.*)

Dunlin

Greenshank   *Curlew*

CORRECTIONS AND OTHER REVISIONS
(MAY 1991)

WALK 2 Page 16: The length of the shorter walk is not 6 miles but 6 km., i.e. just under 4 miles.

WALK 3 Page 21, line 9: for Penhale read Pennance.

WALK 4 Page 25, Section 2: Instead of using the track going left just before the bridge, you could cross the bridge and take the path on the left after a few yards, which is even more attractive. This is the path through Lambsclose Plantation which I refer to below in connection with page 29. Turn right after crossing the stile at the top to continue to Cowlands.

Page 26: It is said that when the rest of Old Kea Church was demolished, the tower was retained because it is a picturesque detail in the view from Tregothnan.

Page 29 Section 11: The route I would now recommend from Roundwood Quay is as follows: As you walk away from the Quay, about 50 yards beyond the metal gate beside the last house turn left up the steps into the wood. Bear right. Soon you come to the inner ditch and rampart of the earthwork. Turn right and follow the curving ditch till you come to a wooden bench. There go right, crossing the outer ditch. At the T-junction, where there is a gate to your right, turn left. Now keep to the main path, which will bring you to the "open field" mentioned on page 29. (Saplings have been planted beside the path there, so it will not be "open" for ever.) Just before the wooden bridge (Section 12), for a delightful short diversion you could take the narrow path on the right (although you may have used it earlier), which runs through the woods (Lambsclose Plantation) with the stream on your left, then emerges into another "open field" where saplings have been planted. Cross the stile, turn left, then left again through the kissing-gate, and follow this track back down, passing above the wooden bridge. Continue ahead for Trelissick.

Page 31 - Short Walk 1: I apologise for giving confusing directions here. For the short way back to Trelissick you do not cross the bridge, but keep to the main path curving right, with Lamouth Creek on your left.

WALK 7 Page 44, Section 3: Please note that there is no public right of way down to Ardevora Veor Farm. The diversion is still worthwhile, though, for the view from the top.

Page 46: "Ardevora" is actually pronounced "Ar-_dev_-o-ra".

WALK 8 Pages 50-1, Section 4: The name of the farm where there is a dispute about right of way is spelt "Nanshuttall". The dispute is still, I am afraid, not settled, so the alternative route described still has to be used at present. (The drawing of St Just Church also needs updating, unfortunately, because the gales of February 1990 destroyed many of the pine trees shown.)

WALK 10: A ferry service from St Mawes to Place (point 5 on this walk) started in May 1991 and will run till 29th September, half-hourly from 10 a.m. to 5 p.m. Let's hope it will be sufficiently well used to continue operating in future years.